CREDIT SCORE SECRETS

HOW TO BOOST YOUR CREDIT SCORE FAST AND LEGALLY, UNDERSTANDING AND BUILDING A GOOD CREDIT PROFILE. HOW TO USE CARDS.

Table of Contents

Introduction 1

Chapter 1. The FICO Scoring Model 6

Chapter 2. The Vantage Scoring Model 17

Chapter 3. What Is Influencing My Score? 22

Chapter 4. 10 Ways to Positively Impact Your Credit Score 30

Chapter 5. What Is A Credit Report? 38

Chapter 6. What is Credit Counselling? 45

Chapter 7. What is the Difference Between a Charge Card and a Credit Card? 51

Chapter 8. How Long Does Negative Information Stay on My Credit Report? 60

Chapter 9. How Do I Increase My Credit Limit? 71

Chapter 10. The Benefits of Good Credit 79

Chapter 11. Goodwill Letter 88

Chapter 12. How Do Credit Cards Work? 92

Chapter 13. Personal or Business Credit Card? 100

Chapter 14. Keeping Your Score Healthy 106

Conclusion 112

Introduction

What is a Credit Score?

The idea of using a mathematical measurement of person's credit file makes sense at some level. We use numbers to measure grades in school, so why not credit? Most young people today have no memory of relationship-based lending. Some readers may remember visiting their local bank to apply for a mortgage or auto loan and discussing their loan with a person, perhaps someone with whom they had a long-established banking relationship. Even such considerations as dressing up and presenting yourself appropriately were all recognized as a large part of getting an approval in the person-to person process. Applying for a loan may have at one time been a close cousin to applying for a job. Now, credit decisions are boiled down to a three-digit number and usually made by a computer, not a human. While converting the subjective world of good and bad credit into a number is innovative and potentially very useful, it also creates a large number of challenges. Who decides how these scores are calculated? What type of credit behavior constitutes good credit and is deserving of a high score? What type of credit behavior constitutes bad credit?

Likewise, we must know the term delinquency which implies the set of overdue credits, and they are considered overdue credits when the date of payment of the installment arrives, these are not cancelled or when they only amortize a part of the amount established as installment.

Understanding the credit system will help you better manage your credit cards, and allow you to profit from them. Understanding how the system works will help you use it to your advantage and allow you to make your credit cards a valuable financial asset which can be used to grow your wealth.

Don't procrastinate on starting the steps to repair your credit. You don't need to wait for years for the negative items to fall off your credit report before you start taking these steps.

It is time for you to stop missing out on the finer things in life simply because of bad. You can use the quick and easy method to remove negative items from your credit report. It gives you step-by-step instructions on what to do to remove negative. You'll find that it's probably easier than you think.

It's important that you understand what you need your credit score for. A good score can help when applying for a mortgage, auto loans, credit cards, business loans and other types of credit. Some strategies, although they do not directly affect your credit score, will help you get a mortgage easier.

It's important to plan ahead for major loans such as mortgages and auto loans. With proper planning ahead of time, you can dramatically raise your credit score using these strategies and make sure to get the best possible rate and terms on your loan. For a mortgage loan, seven years is the ideal time to plan ahead! But even if you don't have the luxury of planning that far in advance, you'll still find these strategies helpful.

A credit score is a numerical expression or a score based on your past credit history which is filed in a credit report. This number represents the credit worthiness of an individual. A credit score is assigned by credit reporting companies like Equifax, Experian and Trans-Union. Most companies use Vantage score for determining the credit score of the consumer but some companies use their own specific calculations for calculating the credit score for the consumer.

How to improve credit score?

There are many things you can do to improve your credit score. Build a good credit history-Credit score is a prediction of your behavior and signifies your credibility to pay back to the lender. If you do not have a credit history there are high chances of the lender rejecting your application. The best way to build a good credit history is by making payments on time and spending within credit limit.

Limit applications filled in a small time frame-The score gets affected if a lot of credit searches show on your file in a small time frame. It is better to limit your applications on loan, credit card, mortgage and more. If you are just trying to get a quote for a loan asked the lender to do a quotation search on tour account rather than a credit search. This will ensure no negative impact on your credit score.

Stability is good if you are home owner, or lived at the same address for a long time, and are employed, it increases the chances of your application of getting approved. Giving your land line number helps in the security check and improves chances of acceptance.

Cancellation of unused credit cards- Its best to limit the number of credit cards used, it helps in maintaining the cards without making any mistake. If you have a credit card you don't use then go ahead and cancel it

Deal with the past defaults- You must try to improve credit score by getting rid of those defaults. Negotiate with the lender that if you pay the debt in full then the details is wiped form your credit report.

Minimize your debt amount- If you have some saving its best to use it to pay your debt and decrease your debt amount. Lenders have access to see the amount of outstanding debt you owe, and will impact their decision.

Chapter 1. The FICO Scoring Model

You have heard it again and again, your FICO score must be so high to get this type of credit, this kind of interest rate, and this type of privilege. The FICO score is the single most important factor that stands between you and just about anything you want to get.

While many people fully understand the impact of the FICO score on their credit, few people, if asked, could tell you what it is or how it is determined. Given the weight that this number holds over so many people, it seems amazing that more people don't ask what it is or what they can do about it. They just simply accept the fact that this number has so much power in their lives.

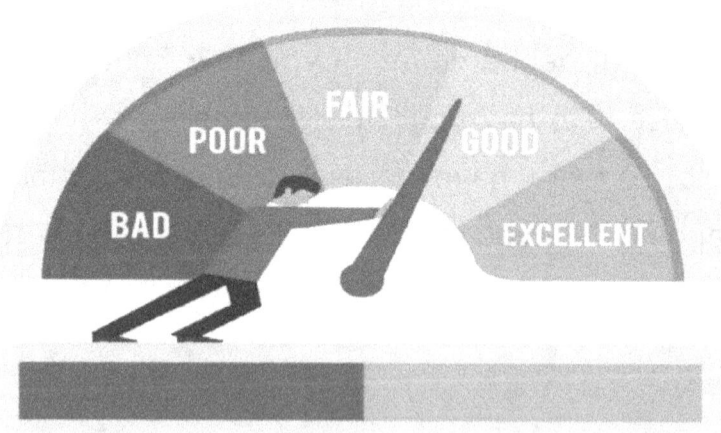

An individual has many credit scores; however, the most prominent of them which is relied on by the majority of lenders is the FICO Score. Being able to comprehend the variables that determine how it is calculated can ensure that you are informed on the actions that either positively or negatively affect your score. When you concentrate on the large things listed below that can positively influence your score, you can make a significant impact for it to rise.

Your credit score is something that can cause a massive transformation in your finances. A good score enables you to access lower interest rates, better credit cards, and it could even aid you when renting an apartment. Nevertheless, not every individual understands how exactly a credit score is formulated or many of the other essential basics of a credit score. Credit scores were designed to allow for easy decision making on the part of lenders. Credit unions and banks typically require information on how much default risk you pose on any loan you are given. This is why they view your borrowing history for signs. For instance, they would like to ascertain if you have borrowed and successfully repaid those loans. They also want to know if you recently stopped paying on numerous loans.

When you apply for a loan, your activity is reported by lenders to credit bureaus, which then transform that information into credit reports. When it comes to credit scores, computer-derived programs can read all of this information and provide a score, which lenders can use to assess your likelihood of repayment. Rather than spending minutes digging through every individual credit report required for a loan, merely looking at the scores allows lenders to have a fast-overall idea of the individual's creditworthiness.

Certain people are without a borrowing history because they are young: they haven't ever taken out a loan or made use of a credit card or any other form of credit. Lenders have to take into account different credit scores for these sorts of applicants. These alternative payment history sources are rent, utility bills, and more.

You can ask for those free credit reports and see what they are reporting about you. You will also see if there are errors and you can correct them so that they do not affect your credit score.

How Is FICO Score Calculated?

If you have ever looked up your credit score, you may have wondered why each major credit bureau showed a different number. In addition to the three major credit bureaus using different methods to calculate credit scores, different lenders and creditors may choose to report to different bureaus.

A certain credit card company might only report to Equifax, while a particular lender might report to TransUnion and Experian. Another lender might not report to any of the bureaus at all. Creditors and lenders can choose to report to them, but it is not required. Payment history doesn't go straight to the credit bureaus by default; it goes to the creditors and lenders, and it will only reach the bureaus if they decide to report it to them. Different companies might prioritize certain things over others. For instance, an auto lender might emphasize a person's payment history, while a mortgage company might place more emphasis on the person's employment history. Other lenders might take a more balanced approach and look carefully at multiple things, prioritizing them equally.

The criteria they have to choose from to calculate your credit score include:

FICO Score - Credit Score -
As calculated

Payment history	35%
Amounts Due (level of indebtedness)	30%
Long credit history	15%

New credits (debts)   10%

Credit Mix   10%

1. Payment History – 35%

The most important component of your credit score looks at whether you've paid your bills on time.

According to FICO, your payment history accounts for 35 percent of your score. Payment history includes information about your account payments, such as the number of accounts you have paid on time and any delinquent payments. To improve this fragment of your credit score, work toward consistently making timely payments for revolving loans, such as credit cards, and installment loans, such as student loans. It is also smart to develop a plan to achieve a goal of debt cancellation.

These are red flags to potential lenders that you might not pay them back.

2. Amounts Owed – 30%

The second-most important component of your credit score is how much you owe. It looks at how much you're using of the total credit you have available – also known as your "utilization ratio."

Less is better, but owing a little bit can be better than owing nothing at all because lenders want to see that if you borrow money, you are responsible and financially stable enough to pay it back. To improve this credit score factor, keep credit card balances low in relation to the available credit, and pay bills on time. If you tend to maximize your credit cards or approach your credit limits every month, lenders will consider it a high risk. It is also useful to find out how much you could have to pay off a credit card before increasing your balances.

3. Length of Credit History – 15%

The duration of your credit history accounts for 15 percent of your FICO score. This includes how long your accounts have been open and the time since your last account activity. A longer credit history gives lenders a better idea of their long-term financial behavior.

If you do not have a credit history, lenders will consider other factors, such as bank accounts, employment history, and residency history. For example, if you have a savings account or checking account in good condition, your bank will be more willing to offer you a credit card or loan. If you still have difficulty obtaining credit, you might consider creating your credit with a secured credit card - which uses the money you put in a secured deposit account as collateral - or an insured loan, which is a loan in which you offer an asset as collateral.

4. New Credit – 10%

Your credit score considers how many new accounts you have applied for recently and when the last time you opened a new account was (opening a bunch at once will hurt your score),

The new loan accounts for 10 percent of your FICO score. This means the number of new requests for new credit, including the number of recent major requests and the number of new accounts you have opened in the last 60-90 days.

Requesting a high number of new credit accounts in a short period of time can have a negative impact on your score. Lenders will consider it a sign of risk. Instead of responding to each card offer with a low-interest introductory rate, apply for new credit only when it makes financial sense for your situation and objectives. And if they deny it, take some time to work towards improving your credit score before requesting it again.

5. Types of Credit In Use – 10%

The final component of your credit score looks at whether you've got a mix of different types of credit (such as a car loan, mortgage, credit cards, store accounts and student loan). Lenders like to know that you can manage different kinds of accounts responsibly.

The different types of credit you use an account for 10 percent of your FICO score. Having a variety of account types, such as credit cards, home loans, and retail accounts, can tell lenders that you have lower credit risk. You can potentially improve your score by opening new types of accounts, but apply for credit only when you need it. Never apply for credit just for the purpose of improving your score.

Credit Score Table:

FICO Score	Meaning
Exceptional	800 or more
Very Good or High	740 to 790
Good	670 to 739
Regular	580 to 669
Bad	579 or less

Are there any other criteria for lending money in addition to the FICO Credit Score?

The lender is free to use the criteria you want. In the USA, 90% of the companies that lend money use the FICO Score. However, who will lend money is who decides what importance it gives to the score.

There are 3 credit reporting agencies: Equifax, Transunion, and Experian. What these companies do is collect and consolidate information about our life in general:

- Where we live

- Where we work

- What do we buy

- Who we are paying (rent, mortgage, stores, etcetera)

- If we have accounts of services or utility accounts (electricity, telephone, water, TV, etcetera)

- If we apply to open any credit card account

- If we apply to any consumer account (furniture, store, etcetera)

- If they lent us money for a purchase, etcetera.
- For how long have we been financially active

Based on that credit report and using a mathematical formula, they calculate our credit score.

Car financing companies are usually more flexible and give credit to people with low scores or recent payment problems. There is more, they change the formula to calculate the score when what will be done is a car loan.

Banks and mortgage companies, on the other hand, are much stricter when lending money. And in addition to asking that we have a certain minimum credit score, they also demand that the credit report be impeccable: no collections (collections), outstanding debts, etcetera.

Many of us have to "fix" the credit report first before we can obtain a mortgage loan.

Are there other Credit Score Tables?

Yes, although 90% use FICO every day, a score called the Vantage Score is being used. This new vantage score is being used by 10% of the companies and they calculate it differently from the FICO score.

Although the Vantage Score is not as popular as the FICO Score, it is important that we keep in mind that they are calculating them. As we see, more and more importance is given to our behavior when it comes to paying bills.

These factors have no influence when calculating your credit score, but your lender can take them into account when approving for a debt. Some are illegal, such as race, religion but nevertheless, they are still used. If you feel you have been discriminated against, there are resources to complain.

Chapter 2. The Vantage Scoring Model

The second main scoring model in use today is the Vantage Score model. The three credit bureaus Experian, Equifax, and TransUnion made a rare show of unity back in 2006 when they decided that they would create a competitor to FICO in an effort to standardize credit scores. The end result was to increase the number of credit scores available to lenders and creditors.

Vantage Score's model considers similar data to FICO but weights them differently. They look at on time payment of your bills, maintaining lower credit card balances, and taking on too many new credit obligations to compile their score. Vantage's primary advantage for people who are new to credit is that they can generate a score for you in as little as two months from your first reported credit card payments.

FICO scores are different from generic credit scores. They apply a proprietary set of algorithms to come up with your credit risk using the information found within your personal credit reports. Other companies will often pattern their credit scores to look as close to a FICO credit score as they can, but as FICO notes1, this can result in scores that are even 100 points apart from the gold standard in the industry.

Even a couple of points can determine whether you get a favorable interest rate and set of terms (saving you as much as thousands of dollars over the term of the loan or credit).

How Is Vantage Score Calculated?

Vantage Score is using similar criteria to weigh your credit worthiness as does FICO. The primary differences are the weighting that they place on the different components and the fact that they pull data from all three credit reporting bureaus in determining your score. We look at their six scoring components.

1. Payment History – Highest Weighting

The top forecaster of risk for you with Vantage Score is your payment history. Their model assigns a 40 percent weighting to this, making it twice as important as their most important category, or as important as the second and third categories combined.

Late payments must be avoided at all costs. These can stay on your credit report for as long as seven years.

2. Age/Type of Credit – Extreme Weighting

This category is the combination of credit history length and your kinds of credit. If you are able to make on time payments on a five year auto loan while you are paying 30 year mortgage payments and monthly credit card bills, then Vantage Score considers you exceptional in this category.

It counts for 21 percent, making it the second most important part of the algorithm.

3. Credit Utilization – Extreme Weighting

To come up with this figure, you simply divide your total balances by your available credit. You should maintain this level at less than 30 percent. Ten percent is even better.

4. Total Balances – Medium Weighting

Vantage Score gives 11 percent weighting to your total debt category (whether it is current or delinquent). By lowering your total debt, you will achieve a higher score in this category.

5. Recent Behavior – Low Weighting

This category gets five percent. It looks into how many recently opened accounts you have as well as the quantities of hard inquiries. It is considered higher risk when you have a larger number of hard inquiries since you could be taking on significantly more debt.

6. Available Credit – Extremely Low Weighting

This category counts for three percent. Available credit refers to the amount in credit that you have available for use at any given point. The more credit you have available, the more points they will assign you in this least important category.

Credit Karma is the biggest name using Vantage Score's model these days. They offer a completely free service (giving you your credit report and a credit score) that is subscribed to by over a hundred million consumers. You can also get credit monitoring from them.

Vantage Score is also on revised versions now. In 2017, they changed their model in the trended data. Now if you are making larger payments to pay down your debt, then you will get more points than an individual who only makes the minimum monthly payments and one who is gradually increasing credit card debt.

Something else that sets Vantage Score apart from FICO and other credit scoring models is that they ignore collections if they are under $250. They also provide dispensation for people who have suffered from natural disasters. Vantage Score also gives a letter grade of A through F alongside their credit score so that consumers are better able to comprehend what their credit score signifies.

Chapter 3. What Is Influencing My Score?

The credit score or FICO score is a score that goes from approximately 300 to 850. That number is calculated using a secret mathematical formula where our behavior is taken into account when paying debts.

The credit score is used by banks, insurers, landlords, employers, companies, in general, to qualify us when they will give us credit, a job or even provide a service.

If my score is high, this tells the lender that I am a responsible person who has historically paid their bills on time. He/she feels calm lending me money because most likely he/she will pay it back.

If on the contrary, I have a bad score, the lender is running the risk that I will not pay him and lose his money. That's why he charges higher interest because apparently, I'm not so responsible with my debts.

Things that do not affect credit:

Building your credit history may not be easy, but it may be harder still to keep it clear.

A survey was recently conducted where they discovered that many people do not know what affects their credit score. For example, the survey revealed that:

- 63% of respondents believe that their income affects the credit score when in reality the income has nothing to do with the credit report.

- 60% of respondents think that work history affects the score. The work history does not influence the credit score at all.

- 53% of respondents think that the amount of savings and money in the bank is proportional to the credit score. Nothing is further from reality.

- 39% of respondents have the mistaken belief that age is a factor that influences credit scores.

Neither the income, nor the work history, nor the savings or the money that is kept in the bank, nor the age are factors that are used to calculate the credit score.

Factors that do, on the other hand:

- 35% of your score depends on your credit history: Or what is the same your debt history. If you do not have debts there is nothing to report, and if there is nothing to report then you have no credit history.

- 30% of the score is based on the debt levels: How much you owe in relation to the credit limit. Having credit and using a certain part of it does not affect your score, but if you have more than 30% of debts in relation to your credit limit, then you begin to affect your score negatively. If your debts go down too much, your score begins to disappear.

- 15% Time: For how long have you had credit. In other words, how long have you been in debt?

- 10% has to do with the type of debt: It is not the same to have a credit card of $ 500 that one with a limit of $ 25,000 or a financed car or a Lease. The more important the debt, the greater the positive impact on the credit score.

- 10% New applications: the last time you applied for the credit. Or what is the same the last time you applied to get into debt.

As you can see, the credit score only measures the capacity and fulfilment of debt payments.

Where Do I Stand With My Credit Score?

There are various ways in which one can look at what a good credit score is or is not. One of such is gauging an individual's credit score as this gives you the ability to properly estimate a borrower's capacity to pay back a loan. If the individual's score is high, this obviously entails that the person can be able to acquire valuable credit and also pay back the funds loaned to them in no time. However, if the score is low, the case is different. As for a low score, lenders will be very cautious of one who seeks a loan and it can be difficult for one to have funds given to them. To the lender's perspective, several scores have different meanings and deductions, based on which scoring system the creditor uses.

Obtaining the valuable credit score goes a long way to make a choice on if the funds should be loaned or not.

This also helps these entities that want to extend credits to know the precise amount of money to give the person as well as with what interest rate.

Experian, Equifax, and TransUnion are the three most common credit reporting agencies. Each of these companies offers a free credit report individually making it a total of three reports per year. From this, you can tell that it is necessary that one reads and understands the contents that are on the report keenly. Information such as errors in the amount of monies to be paid back, payment histories and errors in late payment content can be seen. It also helps to confirm that there is no identity theft in the report.

Companies offering credit will be cautious in taking a closer look at numbers on the credit score of an individual. Lenders believe that a score of 700 or above is a very excellent one. One should value keeping their scores high at all times because there seem to be several advantages of obtaining a high credit number. Credit extensions having low-interest rate offers would definitely be secured by the high scoring report owners. Moreover, for those with high excellent scores, credit approval processes are normally done super-fast (in little or no time).

In the list below, a person can see, through a credit lender's eyes, the information and determine it:

- [ ] 760 or above:- Excellent

- [ ] 700 – 759:- Very good

- [ ] 680 – 699:- Good

- [ ] 620 – 679:- Fair

- [ ] 300 – 579:- Poor

Before applying for a big loan, it is important to note that the one who wants to credit is expected to screen their report at least up to six to twelve months approximately. Checking the report helps you see for yourself that the details are listed correctly and fish out errors that may not seem to tally. In a case where there are errors, the period earlier mentioned allows the one seeking credit to properly address the errors that may have occurred. In a case where errors on the report still surface at the time of applying for a large loan, it is still critical that the lender is made aware of these mistakes depending on the situation.

It is possible to improve on one's credit score. One of the ways this can be done is ensuring you pay all monies owed on a regular basis hence reducing your outstanding account balances. Since deadlines of payments are noted on every report, it is always best to pay in good time. For the borrower's sake, it would be advisable not to take on new debt.

To round this up, here are a few things I'll mention that point you to receiving a good credit score:

Speaking with creditors and credit advisors will be a major advantage for you as there are cases where one might be faced with a really terrible financial crisis where payments cannot be made within that time. The creditors would most likely be ready to assist to the best of their ability especially when it comes to lowering and spreading out payments.

Do not allow your credit card balances go to the roofs. Making them as low as possible is vital. I do not advise you to let them go high.

One thing that makes me laugh about some people is that they think they can improve their credit's score by simply just closing their old accounts so they hide late payments displayed on those accounts. It doesn't work that way. The late payment history will still show on the credit report even if that account is closed.

Lenders always check to see the credit history with active borrowing of last years or more.

Achieving a good credit score range might not be easy at first but it will go a long way to boost your personal financial life. All this must be done with a sense of keen insight as well as with careful thinking.

Chapter 4. 10 Ways to Positively Impact Your Credit Score

The Recency Principle

When calculating your credit score, the most emphasis is placed on recent information. For example, a late payment one month ago has more effect on your score than a late payment a year ago. Therefore, time will gradually repair bad credit; every month that passes helps your score if you pay your bills on time. There are many ways to increase your credit score quickly, but the only way to increase it permanently is to pay your bills on time and let time heal any old wounds such as missed payments or bankruptcy.

Closing Accounts

One way to raise your credit score is by having three to five open credit card accounts, with each of them having very low balances. However, if you already have more than 5 credit cards, don't close any of your open accounts unless the terms are really bad (like a high annual fee). If the terms are bad, instead of closing the account, call the credit card company and ask them to waive your annual fee or give you a different card without an annual fee. Closing an account will lower your credit score by reducing your overall available credit and debt ratios. Therefore, only close your account as a last resort.

Collections

Late payments and collection accounts will significantly lower your credit score. Collections and charge-off are especially damaging. Even after a collection has been paid off with a zero balance, the fact that it is on your report will significantly lower your score for several years. Credit agencies don't look at your payment amount. All they care about is that your payments are on time or not, and how delinquent they were if not paid on time.

Delinquency Severity

Credit agencies measure in 30, 60 and 90 day increments. A 90-day delinquency is far worse than a 30-day delinquency and will lower your score accordingly.

This is why you have to understand how the system works! For example, late payments on a mortgage that are less than 30 days late are not reported. Therefore, it may be better to avoid paying your mortgage and pay your credit cards on time if you can pay the mortgage within that 30-day window. Utility companies do not report late payments, unless of course they turn you over to collections.

Getting An 800+ Credit Score

If you're going for perfect credit and want to maintain a score above 800, ideally you should have only three open accounts. But there are some specialized loans where you would need up to five open accounts with a reporting history of at least 24 months. Having a credit score in the 750 to 780 range is really excellent credit and will generally qualify you for the best rate on any mortgage loan.

Avoid the Credit Limit

High credit balances near the limit will lower your score once you missed a payment. Therefore, it is better to have several accounts with small balances than one or two accounts with large balances. You should maintain all your balances between 0% - 30% of the allowed limit for the best credit score. There is a modest hit to score at a 50% balance compared to the credit limit. There is a major hit to score at a 75% or higher balance. If balances are carried for some time at 75% or higher it will be impossible to maintain a credit score over 700.

Maxing Out

Any account that is maxed out repeatedly month after month will lower your score, even if you pay it off every month without being late or carrying a balance. The credit monitoring system will only recognize balances under 30% at the time your credit is pulled for the best score! The easiest solution is to get a credit limit raised and only borrow up to the 30% limit. Just call your credit card company and most of the time they will gladly raise your credit limit.

Payment History

Credit card payment history (revolving credit) has a heavier weighting on your credit score than installment loans. Therefore, it is better to pay down credit cards before paying down installment or auto loans.

Finance Company Loans

Having a finance company loan on your credit report will lower your credit score even if you pay on time. Having two finance company loans is worse; having three or more is worse still. A regular auto loan is not considered to be in this category. Beware of furniture companies, electronics companies, lumber yards and other companies who set up financing through a 3rd party finance company. These types of loans should only be used as a last resort as they will damage your credit while active even if you pay them on time.

Isolated Event vs. Habitual Offender

One isolated delinquent payment isn't very damaging, but frequent delinquent payments signals a red flag that you are a habitual late payer which will drastically lower your credit score. Also, sporadic late payments (a 30 day late last month and a 30 day late three months ago) are more damaging than successive late payments (successive 30 day late payments are called "a rolling 30" and it counts as only one late payment). This is because, if you're late multiple times in a row, agencies just assume you're going through a tough cash crunch. But if you're late and then on time and then late and then on time, it shows that you have poor financial habits and hurts your score even more.

Tips to raise your credit score

One simple way to improve your credit score is to lower your credit utilization. If you have a low credit limit, however, it can be difficult to keep your spending down 10% - 30% of this limit. Spending close to your limit, even if you pay it off each month, will not help your credit utilization. That's why it's useful to know how to increase your credit limit.

You could increase your overall credit limit by applying for more credit cards, but if you have a few already, it may be better to ask your creditor if they would be willing to increase the limit. If you have been paying in full every month, and have build up a good relationship with your credit card company, they may be willing to help you. This allows you to increase your credit without the hassle of opening new cards and having additional credit inquiries.

The following are some tips for getting your credit score increased:

Don't Ask Too Soon

In most cases, your credit card company is going to automatically check your credit about six months after you opened the account to see how things are going and they may increase your credit at this point. If they do not, however, it's fine to call them and ask them to increase it. You should never ask for an increase before waiting at least six month.

Don't Ask For Too Much

You should be conservative when you ask for a credit increase. It's not a good idea to ask for double or triple your current limit. If you ask for too much, it's likely the credit card company will decline and then you will have to wait some time before asking again. It's best to ask for no more than a 25% increase at one time.

Use Your Card Often

A good way to show the issuer that you deserve more credit is to use your card on a regular basis and pay it in full. This may mean putting a larger balance on the card and then paying it back over a few months. This shows your creditor that you need access to more funds, but that you are still responsible enough to handle larger limits responsibly. The easiest way to do this is to stop paying for things using cash. Instead, put everything you can on your credit card. This allows you to build up a strong history of paying off large balances each month.

Limit Requests

It's not a good idea to ask for limit increases for all your cards at once. This is because each time you make a request, your issuer is going to make a credit inquiry. If the issuer sees a few hits on your report at once, especially from other credit card companies, they will see this as a big red flag. Instead, limit your request to your best credit card company. It is better to make a strong case to just one company, rather than spreading yourself out and trying to convince a bunch of companies. If you do get denied, wait a few months before trying with a different issuer.

Chapter 5. What Is A Credit Report?

A credit report is a detailed report of your credit history. From the moment you apply for a credit card, obtain a loan, or open a utility account, the credit bureaus start collecting information on you and create a credit report based on this information. Lenders are then able to use this report, along with other information that you provide them, to determine your creditworthiness.

The Credit Bureaus

In the United States, there are three major credit bureaus: TransUnion, Experian and Equifax. Each of these companies is responsible for collecting information about all consumers' including personal information, habits for paying bills and other financial data to form credit reports. Your credit report, therefore, is unique to you because your spending habits, credit cards, loans and more will differ from other consumers. The information will be similar, but there can be some slight differences.

Breaking Down Credit Reports

There is actually quite a bit of information on your credit report. First, you will notice that there is a lot of personal information such as your employment history, social security number (to differentiate you from someone with the same name), and your current and last addresses.

In addition to the personal information, the report includes a summary of your credit history. This summary contains data on the number and types of accounts you have, whether they are in good standing or past due, how high the balances are, credit limits they have and dates they were open. They are very comprehensive, but not always accurate.

The report also lists credit inquiries, and may have negative items describing some of your accounts such as collections, charge-off, judgements or liens. These items typically stay on your report for seven years unless you utilize the dispute process. Negative items impact your credit score and give a bad impression when trying to get credit.

Credit Report Access

Any time that you submit an application for credit, signs a rental agreement or obtains a new insurance policy, the creditor, landlord or insurer are legally able to access your credit report. Employers may also request your credit report, but you need to give them permission in writing to access it. Whoever wants to obtain your credit report will need to pay the credit bureaus to access the information.

The following are those who may request access to your credit report:

• Creditors: When you apply for credit, these businesses are allowed to check your report. They can also monitor it once they have given you credit.

• Mortgage Lenders: If you are applying for a loan on a house, the mortgage lender can see some information on your credit report. If the amount borrowed is more than $150,000 they can even see some information that other creditors are not allowed to see because loan balance is so large.

- Landlords: Often times, a landlord will request access to a credit report that tracks your history of renting and whether you typically pay rent and utilities on time or have ever been evicted.

- Utility Companies: These companies are allowed to access your report, but many utility companies are regulated by the state so there could be rules against denying you services even if you have bad credit.

- Student Loan Lenders: Most students will not lose out on students if they have bad credit, but when applying for a PLUS loan, their parents may have their credit checked.

- Insurance Companies: If you are asking for a large policy, life insurance companies can see some additional older information on your credit report.

- Employers: Many employers will take a look at your credit report to evaluate if you're responsible enough for the job.

- Government Agencies: Some government agencies can use your credit report to determine if you are eligible for public assistance, can afford child support or to verify your identity.

- Collections Agencies: Collectors will sometimes look at your credit report to locate you or learn about additional assets you own.

Obtaining Your Credit Report

According to the Fair Credit Reporting Act (FCRA), the credit bureaus are required to provide consumers a copy of their credit report for free once a year. The federal law also entitles consumers to receive a credit report for free if any company takes adverse actions against them. This adverse action can include denial of employment, insurance or credit as well as notices for collections or judgements. The consumer, however, must request the report no more than 60 days from the date when the adverse action occurred. A few additional situations in which you will be able to obtain a free credit report include times when you are on welfare or unemployment and if you're a victim of identity theft.

Understanding Your Report

Generally, your credit report is divided into four parts. The first part contains all of your personal information including your social security number, name and addresses. The second part is the bulk of the report, and has most of your credit history data. This includes any lines of credit or other debt you currently have.

What is a good score?

Your credit score is split into several levels, but generally ranges from 300 to 850. The different credit rating levels are label as follows:

- 300 to 600: Bad Credit
- 600 to 649: Poor Credit
- 650 to 699: Fair Credit
- 700 to 749: Good Credit
- 750 + 850: Excellent Credit

The higher your credit score, the better. Better scores allow you to get credit easier, and with lower interest rates. Even when not getting credit, such as when you are renting an apartment, having a better credit rating builds trust with potential landlords.

The best thing that you can do to get your credit score up is to make payments on time. As soon as you start missing payments, your score will plummet. A delinquency can turn into a negative item that is much harder to remove. If you do miss payments, communicating and maintaining a good relationship with your creditor is key.

Can I Check My Credit Score for Free?

Check through your bank or your credit card issuer

This score can be found when you are logging into your online account, it is often listed in the statement segment – though may vary from companies to companies.

Buy your credit score

You can decide to buy a credit score directly from the credit reporting companies – you can decide to get it from the source itself. All you have to do is to visit the official website, set up your account, provide details of your personal information, pay the required fee and view your score.

Use a free credit score service

Many websites and platforms provide free credit score services that is designed to enlighten the borrower on the general idea of credit score. Some of these free websites offer educational scores that provide you an insight of your credit score though it may be slightly different from what a lender will see.

Chapter 6. What is Credit Counselling?

At times, an individual might be faced with critical financial instability, especially when his debts are out of control. Faced with such a menace, it is advisable to take time and think of the right solution to the situation. One can even seek for advice in order to reach a decision that will not cost him. The possible remedies in the market include visiting credit counselors and debt-consolidators. Both methods are common in that they will help you to contain the situation. Nevertheless, you need to weigh both options to ensure that you choose the right one depending on the weight of your financial situation.

Credit counselors, these are professionals who will assist you to untangle your financial woes on daily basis. Individuals running these counseling firms have deep knowledge in debt management and other options that can be applied to minimize debts. Credit counselors provide several alternatives, after which the borrower can manage his debts afterwards.

With the help of the expert, the borrower prepares a realistic budget. This budget stresses mainly on how the borrower spends his money. By the time the counseling process is over, the borrower will come into terms with what exactly caused the debt. The Credit counselors will help the borrower to diagnose the cause so that he will not repeat the same mistake once again. The budget created eliminates any unnecessary expenditure as well as setting tough look at the spending habits of the borrower.

The Credit counselors afterwards supply the borrower with possible options to eliminate all the financial obligations facing him or her. Some of the possible options are learning on debt management, debt consolidation, personal bankruptcy and enlightenment on how to settle ones debt. Basically, the choice of these options will be catalyzed by the severity of debt facing the borrower.

Generally, credit counselors will only enlighten a borrower on how to contain any debt menace on their own. These methods are effective when one is not faced by fatal punishments such as loosing possession of his assets. In such situations, it is advisable to visit debt-consolidators.

Debt-consolidator, although common with credit counselors in that they help borrower contain debt menace, they specifically save borrowers from losing their property or from running bankrupt. Plans given by Debt-consolidator will give a borrower financial freedom within a short period.

Debt-consolidators will require the borrower to have good credit rating in order to qualify for their plans. If one qualifies for the consolidation plans, Debt-consolidators will extend consolidation loans to them. Basically, these are loans inclusive of all the current balances the borrower has not been able to meet. The consolidation of loans relieves the borrower from any current debt obligation, hence good for someone close to losing his personal assets to an unpaid lender.

For a borrower to make the right choice, he needs to weigh to benefits and limitations of each option. For example, debt management might affect future reputation in that lenders might be reluctant in giving the borrower loan as he is presumed to be irresponsible; debt settlement might not be effective in clearing the whole portion of the loan amount hence impairing the borrower's credit rating while the price of debt consolidation is an increased debt for settlement of the current debt.

When it's Time to Seek Counseling

So how exactly do you know when it's time to seek out help? Well essentially there are 3 stages of recovery that you should think about. Stage 1 is self-help. Your credit card and other debts are in such a way that you can essentially take care of it yourself through using credit elimination tactics and making small, logical decisions on how to save money and pay off debts. Stage 2 is when your debts become unmanageable and you decide you need outside help; that's where credit counseling agencies come into play. Stage 3 is when even your outside help doesn't know what to do and your only logical recourse is to file for bankruptcy.

It is probably time to go to credit counseling if you can't control your debt. If you can't make your payments or you know you can't pay off your debt without help, you need this type of counseling. Don't be afraid to answer your phone because it may be collectors calling. Don't struggle to pay all your bills. Don't accept that you will be in debt the rest of your life. Go to credit counseling.

Going to this type of counseling is better than living in fear, in debt, or filing for bankruptcy. Credit counselors may be able to negotiate with credit card companies and get interest lowered or late fees forgiven. It is not guaranteed, but you can certainly try to find a counselor that can do so. A credit counselor will also help you figure out a budget after they look at how much you make, how much your debt is, and how much your utility bills are. Following a counselor's advice and sticking to a budget is really important when trying to get out of debt. It may be difficult, but you will have an amazing feeling when you have no more debt.

Credit counselors are not there to judge you, it is their job to help you. Get counseling recommendations from your bank, credit card companies, or a friend. Make sure a credit counselor is certified. You want a professional that knows exactly what they are doing.

Seeking credit counseling is a huge step to recovering from debt. It is the right thing to do if you have gotten in way over your head. Living in debt is not fun and credit counseling can help you.

That being said, if your debt is actually manageable then you could just be wasting a lot of money by hiring a debt settlement or debt counseling company. In the long run it could save you a lot of money.

Chapter 7. What is the Difference Between a Charge Card and a Credit Card?

Charge Cards

Similar to a credit card in every way, except that they require you to pay the balance in full every month. These cards generally charge an annual fee, because they don't make money from interest fees.

There are many benefits to using a charge card.

First, historically speaking, charge cards don't show on your personal credit report. No balance to report means it won't hurt your debt utilization.

Another benefit to using a charge card is protection for your purchases. If you place an order with your charge card and it arrives damaged, or significantly different than advertised, just call your lender and have the charges reversed.

Besides protecting your purchases, you are also personally protected. A charge card is far better than paying with your debit card.

Credit Card

The credit cards are used as an option of payment in many occasions, but this one should not replace the traditional forms of payment as it is it the cash, nor much less to be used of unrestrained form, since as we use the available line of credit it will become a debt to pay, that will be able to be collected of direct form or in installment, this according to the percentage value of the rate of interest of purchases emitted according to the tariff of the bank. It is very important to know that shopping interest rates are very different from cash withdrawal interest rates, that only some cards usually have this option.

You must be very aware that credit cards are not salary extensions or additional money, they are a method of payment that provides benefits and like any financial instrument, has a cost and a high responsibility that must be assumed by the card holder. The secret of success is to have a clear debt capacity. For many, plastic is the beginning of their credit life, so keeping a good record (making smart use of your credit) is important to their work, family and financial lives.

The best and most responsible way to use a card is to have knowledge of several important points when you acquire or plan to have one:

Know the billing cycle:

When making an evaluation to acquire a credit card, the bank official has the duty to ask you the days in which you have economic solvency, that is to say, you have the possibility to make the payments corresponding to the debt that you have accumulated using the card and according to it advise you to know which day will be your date of invoicing and an approximate of the dates of payment.

Know your credit card rates:

Depending on the type of card and category you have, depending on your financial solvency, you will need to know the annual and monthly interest rates. This will serve as a guide, to know if you will place your purchase directly or in installment.

It is advisable, not to place low amounts or easy to pay in installment, since for each installment a monthly interest is generated, that at the end of accounts the value of the acquired product costs you the double. Also, to know that if you place a product with the commitment to pay it directly or in a single installment, this means, without generating any interest. You will have to pay it on the agreed date because otherwise, you will incur in arrears, this interest will generate deferred interest which, according to the tariff, may be higher than the interest rate of purchases.

To know the amount of the penalty in case of default:

When you default on the payment date, interest will be added according to the bank in which you belong, since this is usually a percentage of the minimum quota, having a range of the minimum and maximum amount to be charged.

Know the annual membership to pay or the minimum consumption amount for the exoneration:

Some credit cards do not charge annual membership, but others do, in this case, you should know with what amount you can avoid paying the membership, which can be considered as payment for using the brand of the card and its various benefits it brings with it, always consider the type of plan and service are those you need when acquiring a credit card best suited to your pace of life.

To know the tax-deductible insurance that banks charge monthly on a mandatory basis:

This is only in the event of death or any accident or illness that makes it impossible for you to carry out the basic or work functions that allow you to support yourself financially, i.e. when you cannot generate income to cancel your payments, a direct relative may request information from the bank about the tax deduction insurance and how to exercise it, in order to assume the expenses of the person holding the credit card.

Keep track of credit card expenses:

You can do this by having your account statements printed out or by using an Excel spreadsheet. If you receive your EECC by email, we often receive so much information that we cannot see the EECC on time, it is usually also the most economical way, because the shipment has an extra cost, but what can be considered to avoid this, is to have a scheduled date to print or make the Excel table. This should be considered about 5 days after your billing date because the day you bill your card is the day the bank will collect your purchases at your EECC and specify it in the system.

Don't overshoot:

Keep in mind that some credit cards have the option of being overdrawn, to know more detail of it, you must know your available credit line and have control of your expenses. The overdraft can sometimes save you when you don't have enough money to be able to buy something, but then in your EECC, you will be able to see the charge for it and the interest charged by the entity.

Don't spend more than you earn:

Despite the fact that you place the consumption in installment, you have already used a large amount of your credit line and in case of an emergency, you will not have the economic solvency to pay the full amount invoiced in your card and the emergency.

According to these points already exposed, one can have an order when buying a product with a credit card, however we must not only consider it, but we must be very careful with the use of this plastic so well known by fraudsters.

Usually, the main security measures you should have are the following:

Only the credit card holder should know the PIN for cash withdrawals or when requested to do so by an establishment.

Do not lose sight of your credit card, as it is enough to know your full details, the expiration date of the card and security code to be able to make an online purchase in a store or register it in an application.

If your card gets lost, it's a good idea to block it immediately, even though it's just a loss, a credit card in the wrong hands can make endless purchases in minutes.

If you visualize in your EECC a consumption that you don't recognize, you must block your card and issue a claim for unrecognisable consumptions to the bank, according to the estimated term for a claim, they will carry out the verifications and they will send you a notification or letter of answer, giving to know the detail of the consumption and answer of the case, of not being satisfied with the answer issued by the bank, you can make an appeal.

To deactivate the option of purchases by the Internet of your credit card, this prevents that although they know third people your data and information of your card, the same system of the bank prevents that the purchases are made. The only person authorized to activate this option is the holder and with the appropriate recognition measures to do so.

It is recommended that if you travel, you activate it with exact dates and mentions that register the countries in which you will use the card.

Types of Credit Card

There are several types of credit cards, starting with the world's leading payment brands, as they are:

- Visa
- Mastercard
- American Express
- Diners Club

And also, according to the category of credit card you acquire, according to your monthly income, the most common are:

- Classic
- Gold
- Platinum
- Signature
- Infinite

But as demand for these cards grew, each leading payment brand created new versions of these card categories, being unique and with different features and benefits.

Chapter 8. How Long Does Negative Information Stay on My Credit Report?

If there is damaging information in the report, you have the right to dispute that information. They must reinvestigate the items in question within a "reasonable period of time". If a disputed item cannot be verified, they must remove it from your file.

Never Use The Online Dispute System: This leaves you without the paper trail you will need if the credit bureau doesn't follow the law.

Be sure to use certified mail whenever you are sending a letter to the credit bureau - to ensure that they receive it and that you have proof of receipt.

Do not dispute more than 22 items at a time. It is extremely important to follow proven procedure. Credit bureaus are looking for any excuse not to investigate your dispute.

Hard Inquiry: Two Years

Too many hard inquiries on the report may lead to a low credit score. A hard inquiry will only be on the report for two years following the inquiry date.

Delinquency: Seven Years

Make your payments on time, or you can catch up. If you usually repay your debt, call your creditors and ask that the delinquency should not be reported to a credit company.

Charge-Off: Seven Years

Make sure to pay all the debt or the negotiated amount

Student Loan Default: Seven Years

Take advantage of the Department of Education options loans such as repayment, consolidation, and rehabilitation when on federal student loans. When on private loans, get across to your lender and ask for modification.

Foreclosure: Seven Years

Make it a commitment to pay all your bills on time and rebuild the credit.

Judgment or Lawsuit: Seven Years

Make sure that your credit report public records do not have information about civil judgments, and if it does ask for the removal.

Bankruptcies: Seven Years

Collect secured credit card from your lender and clear your bankruptcy accounts and apply for another credit once you have cleared the debt.

Tax Lien: Indefinitely before, now Zero years

Make sure your credit report does not have information about tax liens. If you discovered that your credit report has tax liens, request for it to be removed by your agency.

Just note that the negative information will be removed once the credit reporting time has been reached. If they are not removed, you have the chance to dispute it with the credit company involved.

How To Fix The Negative History

Negative items on the credit reports are indications of consumer's past financial mistakes or mistakes from business or credit bureaus for the errors. No matter where the fault comes from, it is the responsibility of the consumers to make the credit reports favorable.

The following are some of the steps necessary to help in getting better credit by removing negative history from your credit report.

1. Submit the Dispute to the Credit Bureaus

A federal law known as the Fair Reporting Act defines the kind of information that can be on the credit report and for how long it will remain (mostly seven years). The FCRA act stipulates that consumer has the right to an accurate report, so because of this, a consumer has the opportunity to dispute errors with the credit bureaus.

If you want to dispute a negative item through mail, write a letter that describes the credit report attached copies of proof. The bureaus will investigate the dispute with the business that submitted the negative item, and the bureaus will remove the item once it is being confirmed to be error indeed.

The moment the business discovered that indeed there is an error on the credit report, they will send the outcome to the credit bureau for the mistakes to be removed from the credit report.

3. Pay for Delete Offer to the Creditor

The way you have to approach the reported negative information that is accurate is different. The credit bureaus will not remove accurate, verifiable information even if disputed. However, you may need to negotiate for some items to be removed from the credit report.

A technique known as pay for delete offers can be used with delinquency, accounts, or missed payments. In this technique, you agree to pay the bill in full, so for the negative details to be removed from the credit report.

4. Request for Deletion

With the offer of pay for delete, you have the

chance to make use of money as the bargaining power to remove the negative information from the credit report. If the debt has been paid, there is no longer bargaining power, but you have the opportunity to request a goodwill deletion.

Your request letter to the creditor will have the reason there was lateness, how credible you were, and request for the accounts to have a more favorable report. Though some creditors will agree, some won't comply, and some will help in deletions if the right persons handle the request.

5. Wait until the Credit Reporting Time Limit

If all attempts fail, the only chance left is for you to wait for the negative items to get out of the credit report. Don't forget that the Federal law only allows the negative information on the report for seven years. The exception to this law is bankruptcies that can last for ten years. Another good news is that the older the negative items on the credit report, the lesser it will affect the credit score and be replaced with positive items.

6. Things that Don't Work

Some attempts, like filling bankruptcies in helping to remove negative information from the credit report. Even if your debts are discharged in bankruptcy, the balances will be on the report as $0. However, the accounts will still be on the credit report. And all accounts that were in the bankruptcies will also be noted.

Another attempt that won't remove the delinquency reporting is closing an account. The closing account that has past due balance will not remove the report but will report it as delinquent until the debt is paid. Just note that the only benefit of closing an account is you won't be able to use the account

Clearing a delinquent balance will not eliminate the negative items on the credit report. The moment you pay the balance, the account status will bear Current or OK in as much as the account is not collections or charged off.

How Do I Get Credit When No One Wants to Give it to Me?

In an ideal world, financial institutions would only lend to people with great credit. Thankfully, we do not live in an ideal world, but in a world that is driven by markets.

There are a lot of people in the same boat as you and may have faced foreclosures, have declared bankruptcy, or otherwise, ran into serious financial troubles in the past. You are hardly alone. In fact, there are millions of people in the same boat.

This is, of course, a tremendous market opportunity. Whenever there is a huge level of demand, you can rest assure that there will be providers stepping up to meet that demand. The finance industry is no exception. There are financial institutions that specialize in individuals with less than stellar credit.

Huge Opportunity For Lenders

The reason why there are many lenders looking to provide loans to people with bad credit is that it is a tremendous opportunity for them. You have to understand that borrowers differ from each other.

Just because you have a bad credit, it does not necessarily mean that you cannot pay off your loans. In fact, the majority of people with bad credit simply made a mistake in the past. They are, not only willing to pay regularly on any new loans that they take out, but they are also perfectly capable. The only difference between them and so called "good risks" are their credit scores. These people are simply looking for a second chance.

Online Bad Credit Resources

Now that we have established that there are many lenders out there that are willing to extend a loan to you even though you have a bad credit score or bad credit history. Many of these bad credit lenders are available online. They have websites that allow you to apply online. At the very least, they have an online presence that would give you the information that you would need so that you can apply off line. Regardless, you should not overlook in using the internet to find bad credit lenders. There is quite a number of them.

Among the online choices that you will come across, you will probably notice that these financial institutions often fall into three general camps. In reality, they are actually very diverse. In many cases, they are unique from each other.

Don't Forget About Your Local Financial Institutions

If you are looking for a loan, never underestimate local institutions. You might think that all of your best bets are online. Not necessarily. In many cases, local banks and credit unions have special programs for people with less than stellar credit. Never write off local sources of financing.

Local Banks

In your local area, there might be purely local or regional banks. Check them out. A lot of them have websites or, at the very least, you can give them a call and ask them if they have special programs that focus on local lenders with bad credit. You would be surprised as to what you can find. There is a tremendous amount of local flexibility. The more local the bank, the higher the likelihood that you can get a deal.

However, with a purely local bank, you might be able to increase your chances because local banks are purely local. Meaning, they are incorporated locally and exist to serve the needs of local borrowers. They have a lot more leeway in which to operate, in terms of loan approvals, as well as standards.

Credit Unions

If you are a member of a credit union, you might be able to get some special deals. Again, it depends on your particular set of circumstances and also on how severe your bad financial mistakes were. Regardless, do not cross credit unions off your list prematurely.

Call around and check out which available programs are realistic options for you. You might want to look at specific details and for special time sensitive deals. In some cases, credit unions are maybe willing to extend bad credit loans for relatively short periods of time. Regardless, do not expect the interest rates to match those with people with good credit.

Picking The Right Deal

Ideally, you should be entertaining as many different options as possible because the more options that you have on the table, the higher the likelihood that you would make the right choice.

They key here is to be as thorough as possible because you have to remember that this is your chance to get your credit up and going again. You need the very best loan vehicle for that. Picking the wrong deal might derail your plans.

Chapter 9. How Do I Increase My Credit Limit?

One of the least utilized strategies for lowering your debt utilization is a credit limit increase.

All you need to do is call your lender and ask if a credit limit increase is available for your account. Most people don't know that a customer service representative will pull up your entire account before they even answer the phone. They use caller ID to identify you, then have you prove your identity. Once proven, they have all your past conversations, your limits, balances, and possible upgrades available.

They just won't tell you unless you ask. By requesting a credit limit increase you're effectively increasing your available credit without increasing your balance.

For example, if you have one card with a $500 limit and $250 balance, then you're at 50% utilization.

If you get a $500 limit increase, then you have $1000 limit with a $250 balance. That brings your utilization down to only 25% instantly!

The lower your utilization, the higher your scores. With a secured card you simply increase your deposit.

For a regular credit card, make sure you make timely payments for at least 6 months, though 9 months is better. Make sure you keep your card under 50% utilization on all your cards. They won't approve you if you're maxed out or have missed payments within the past year. If they ask you what you're going to use the money for, don't say gambling, or anything irresponsible.

Say you're trying to improve your FICO scores or that you just got a raise and wanted to buy some new furniture. If they ask how large an increase you would like, ask them how much you qualify for. They can tell you after a minute or so.

If you're approved, then you just raised your credit scores with a phone call.

Become an Authorized User

A very simple yet effective technique for boosting your credit scores it to "piggyback" on someone else's credit history and become an Authorized User (AU) on their account.

An AU account is not like a Joint Account.

With a Joint Account both you and the primary holder can add to the credit balance, but you're also both liable for the debts.

If, for example, the primary files for bankruptcy protection, then you will be on the hook for the full balance.

You should avoid Joint accounts at all costs.

With an Authorized User account, only the primary card holder is liable for the debt.

However, the trade line appears on BOTH credit reports.

This is a great way to start your children's credit education, too.

The overnight addition to a credit's age, limit, and payment history can boost a score hundreds of points.

AU accounts are so effective for boosting credit scores that many unscrupulous credit services actually sell them as "Seasoned Trade lines".

First of all, buying a trade line for the purpose of qualifying for financing, like a home mortgage, is fraud. You could go to jail or receive a hefty fine.

Second, FICO knows about Seasoned Trade lines and has made adjustments. When those adjustments hit the scoring model lenders use, then those trade lines will become worthless.

Third, you don't need to buy trade lines anyway. Simply ask a family member, or someone you've shared an address with, to add you as an AU.

Tell them you don't need or want a card, but you want your credit score to benefit from their good credit history.

Look for a card from a major lender with a high limit, low balance, and perfect payment history. The older the card the better.

Refinance Revolving Debt

Any time you pay off your credit cards your score is going to go up.

Refinancing your revolving debt with an installment loan is a way to game the system into thinking you have less debt.

FICO doesn't give as much weight to installment loans, so adding the equivalent installment debt while paying off revolving debt will have an overall positive effect on your score.

Just don't go running up your cards while you're paying off your installment loan or you'll end up with twice the debt.

That's a recipe for disaster.

Day 16 - Refinance Revolving Debt With a Home Equity Loan

Using a Home Equity Loan (HEL) to pay off your revolving debts will improve your credit scores for the same reason using any other installment loan to pay off your revolving debt would work.

FICO gives less weight to installment loan debt.

You just need to make sure you use a Home Equity LOAN and not a Home Equity Line of Credit (HELOC).

A HELOC is scored just like a credit card by FICO, so using it wouldn't improve your scores.

Just be sure to use it to pay down your debt and not as a way to get yourself into more debt.

If you're not disciplined enough to not run up your balances again, then this would not be a smart move for you.

I include it because it works, but you have to pick and choose what works for YOU.

Credit Builder Loans

Some lenders offer a secured loan program designed to help you rebuild your credit.

They're called Credit Builder Loans.

This is a very effective, all be it slow, method for boosting your scores. It's slower because it's an installment loan. Installment loans have less of an impact on your credit score.

Be that as it may, over 6-12 months you will see a credit score increase. That's because you need a few installment loans to improve the "Credit Mix" which is responsible for 10% of your credit score.

Here's how your scores are determined:

FICO SCORES IMAGE

Ideal ratio is:

2-4 credit cards

A car loan, home loan, and personal loan

1-2 retail cards

The credit builder loan completes the personal loan portion of the equation.

Here's how it work;

The amount you borrow is deposited into an escrow account. You can't touch it until the loan is paid. You make your regular payments each month, building your credit score as you go. When you're done paying, you get the full balance plus interest, to do with as you please.

Traditional features include:

Loan amounts from $500-$3000

12-24 month terms

Loan funds earn dividends

Loan interest rate is fixed at 5%

So, for example, a $1000 loan at 5% over 18 months would equal payments of $57.79.

The terms may change from bank to bank so you need to shop around.

Chapter 10. The Benefits of Good Credit

A person with a bad credit score can still obtain credit but may feel the consequences are too much. A poor credit score will result in high-interest rates that can quickly become expensive, especially if you take longer to pay your accounts. A good, excellent, or exceptional credit score will reduce the interest charges and help you to save money in the long run. There are many other benefits to having a good credit score.

Lower Interest Rates

Any person who has credit will need to pay interest on the outstanding account balance. The amount you borrow is often referred to as the capital balance. The balance outstanding is equal to the interest charges and the capital balance together. You can see interest as the profit the lending company gets for giving you credit; some places call it a financing cost. It is a fee that is levied every month in proportion to the amount of credit you have used and not yet paid back. A poor credit score will result in a higher interest rate and thus having to pay more fees. The advantage of a good credit score is a lower interest rate and pay fewer fees.

The lower interest cost makes it easier to pay back your capital balance. Most people are only paying back interest and then have the interest charged again on a monthly basis, which results in a vicious circle of only paying the interest. If you are only paying interest then it is difficult to pay back the capital balance you have borrowed. The better credit score and result in a lower interest rate can work to your advantage. It makes it possible to pay both interest and capital balance and in that way reduce your total debt.

Negotiating Possibilities

A high credit score provides leverage for negotiation. Your bank may have offered you a credit card with a set interest rate. You can approach other financial institutions and find out if they can give you a more favourable interest rate. This negotiating power helps you to find the best possible interest rate and offers with the lowest costs.

Having assets in your name will give you even more negotiating power. Lenders will always choose a customer who has security when it comes to providing credit facilities. Owning an apartment, vehicle, or other assets will give banks the knowledge that you can pay them back. Stable assets help in negotiations with financial institutions for decreasing interest rates and down payments. You should be proud of your high credit score and can always use it as leverage. Many people are scared to negotiate, but it can save you a bucket load of money in the long run. For example, an interest rate that is just 1% lower than the original quoted rate can reduce your total repayment with thousands of dollars. This money could be used in so many other ways than paying off a mortgage.

Improved Chance of Credit Approval

A better credit score makes it easier to be approved for further credit in the future. Every time you apply for credit, the financial institution will do a credit check. Your credit score is then made available to the company that made the request. The credit score will be used to help make a decision on whether the account should be opened, a credit card is issued, or a loan application approved.

Most people with a high credit score will qualify for a home loan or already have a home loan. Ensuring you make frequent payments on your mortgage can greatly contribute to a higher credit score, which will bring additional benefits. If you ever get to a point where you want to do renovations or need additional money, you can visit your home loan company and ask to refinance your home. This means that you will have funds made available to you but your mortgage will increase. You can still negotiate for good interest rates and lower fees. Plus, your long standing relationship with the lender makes it easier to approach them for additional financing.

Great Credit Card Offers

Financial institutions want to work with customers who pay their bills every month. Your credit score is one of the things that is appealing to banks. Many banks will pull credit score information to find potential clients. The bank will then contact you and offer you some great credit card deals. Your own bank is also likely to provide you with better credit terms. If you get a call from a financial institution offering to provide you with a beneficial credit card, then you are most likely doing a great job with keeping your credit score high. Listen to the offer and ask the contact person to send you more information via email. You can then check the options and decide if this credit card is a good idea.

A solid credit score will lead to offers of credit cards with good rewards and other benefits. Some lenders will provide a credit card account to you without charging any monthly fees. Other institutions have rewards programs linked to the credit card. Using your credit card responsibly and for certain transactions will give you points or a specific reward's level. A higher score will qualify you for more rewards. The rewards can include reduced prices on air-plane tickets or discounted rates on accommodation. Some financial institutions will add extra insurance cover, roadside assistance, or a personal banker to take your calls at any time of the day.

Better Insurance Rates

Car insurance is very important to protect you in the case of an accident, whether it is your fault or not. Automotive insurers look closely at credit scores when determining insurance premiums. The same goes for home owner's insurance. You need to have insurance to cover costs should your property ever sustain any damage. A person with a low credit score is perceived to be a high-risk client. The insurance company assumes that these people are more likely to claim from the insurance for unnecessary or fraudulent claims. This lack of trust results in higher insurance premiums.

A similar concept to the credit score is an insurance score used in some companies. The scores are not exactly the same but the general principle of a higher score is better stays the same. Your credit score will greatly influence your insurance score. People with a high credit score are seen as more trustworthy by the insurance companies. They benefit from lower insurance premiums thanks to a good credit record. Additionally, insurance claims may be paid more easily if you are in an accident or have damage to your home. After a claim, your insurance provider may increase the monthly premium to help cover some additional costs and to decrease risk. A higher credit score can be used to help negotiate a lower premium. Always ask your insurance provider to take your credit record into consideration when calculating your monthly premiums and excess amounts.

Better Rental Agreements

Landlords who rent out the property are always concerned about receiving their rental income. Many times a landlord will advertise an apartment but they don't know the people who eventually rent from them. Your credit score is one way for the landlord to learn more about prospective tenants. The landlord or rental agency will often use your credit report to see if you pay on time or miss payments. Often times, landlords are more willing to let property to people with a high credit score and will out rightly reject applicants with a low credit score. A person with a good credit score is more likely to be approved for renting property since the landlord knows that the person is likely to pay.

Landlords are more open to working with people who have a high credit score, which makes the rental relationship much easier. For example, a person with a high credit score may be able to negotiate for a lower security deposit, or even have the possibility of paying the security deposit over a two-month period rather than paying the full amount at once. On the flip side, a person with a low credit score will most likely be asked to pay a substantially higher security deposit.

Fewer Security Deposits

A security deposit is often requested by companies as it shows that you will pay your account in the future. If you do not make payments, then the credit provider can use the security deposit to recover some of the costs. Security deposits are used by companies that provide both products and services.

Cellphone companies often require a security deposit since the customer gets the phone before full payment has been received by the company. This situation is very risky for cellphone providers. The security deposit can cover some of the costs if a person stops paying their cellphone account. Other companies that may require a security deposit are those which offer utilities, such as gas and water. A person with a high credit score often has the benefit of not paying a security deposit or paying significantly less. Your credit history and credit score have proven that you pay your bills on time and provides peace of mind for the company.

Self-Confidence

One of the biggest benefits of a good credit score is the boost your self-confidence experiences. You should be proud of yourself for saving your money and using your credit wisely. A good credit score takes time and effort to achieve. Achieving a high rating deserves a pat on the back. You also know that you can easily use your finances responsibly in the future.

Chapter 11. Goodwill Letter

A Goodwill letter is a request you make to a creditor based on your past and future relationship. Below is an example of a goodwill letter you can use:

Date:

Name of Credit Bureau

Address of Credit Bureau

City, State, Zip

To Whom It May Concern:

I am writing this letter in hope of getting some assistance with my account number. I am hoping to have an adjustment made out of "Goodwill" on my credit report regarding the late payments that were made on this account. I take full responsibility for my actions. At the time of the late payments I was experiencing a financial hardship and since then I have been consistent with my payment obligations with the company.

I am a loyal satisfied customer with the company and will continue to be long into the future. Based on my past and current payment history it shows that outside of this time period I have always made my payments on time. I would greatly appreciate it if you would consider removing the negative marking that are being report to the credit bureaus. I look forward to hearing back from you as soon as you have made your decision. Thank you so much for your attention to this matter at it is of great importance to me.

Sincerely,

Name:

Address:

Phone number:

If the good will letter fails, then you can try disputing.

Hardship Letter

Think of a hardship letter as an extreme goodwill letter. This letter Is used when you have several late payments or are behind on payments and can bring the account current.

In essence, you are asking for a little compassion. Terrible things happen all the time but we all need a break now and again.

Here is a sample letter:

Dear [creditor],

I have recently suffered a serious financial hardship when {spouse died, medical emergency, job loss, business failure, natural disaster... describe the hardship here in moderate detail.}

As a result of this hardship, I have fallen behind on my account with you and would like to do what I can to remedy the situation.

I have {x} late payments on my credit report as a result of this. I am writing to ask, as a matter of good faith, if you would remove the late payments on this account if I can bring the account current and pay all associated late fees.

I would like to salvage my credit and my relationship with you as a creditor as I've been a loyal customer for {x} years!

Any help you can provide or any other options you may have are very much appreciated.

Sincerely,

Customer

While we tend to think of lenders as big uncompassionate machines we need to remember that there are caring and feeling people running those machines.

People can be reasoned with provided you have a real hardship.

Besides, lenders don't make money by sending your account to collections. You just have to give them a reason to work with you and you might be surprised by the results.

Chapter 12. How Do Credit Cards Work?

In order to obtain a credit card, the consumer needs to fill-in an application form that is actually like an agreement between the supplier and the consumer. The credit card supplier approves the application form and provides the consumer with a small piece of plastic which is the credit card. It contains electronically encoded security information in the form of a magnetic strip which is generally located at the back of the credit card. This information is used for authorizing payments whenever the consumer uses the credit card. The consumer can use the credit card for shopping at merchant outlets or on the internet. Credit cards with an interest-free period often have high annual rates. But if you pay your debt within the interest-free period you will avoid paying interest so the higher rate may be worth it.

To make a payment using a credit card, it has to be either swiped into special credit card processing machine or the details of the credit card have to be entered on the merchant's website when shopping online. The credit card supplier sends across the bill for these transactions to the consumer who is then required to pay either the full amount or a partial minimum amount. If you pay in full, the credit card supplier doesn't charge any interest on the amount you owe otherwise the pre-agreed interest rate is charged. If you don't pay even the minimum, you might land up with a late fee too. The credit card supplier generally puts a limit on the maximum amount you can spend per month using your credit card.

The use of credit cards are very important in fixing, rebuilding or improving your credit score, most individuals will suggest that surely credit cards will negatively impact a person's credit score however its has been proven that a very efficiently used credit card will improve your credit score, there are many credit cards companies out there that offers high interest rate credit cards for individuals with bad credit. This is a great opportunity to fix and improve your credit score in order to ensure that your credit card limit is being used efficiently you should only use 25% of your credit limit on a monthly basis and ensure that a repayment is made the following month and absolutely and at all costs avoid late payments and fees as these will negatively impact your credit score.

How To Use Credit Cards to Build Credit

Reward Schemes

It is important to note that credit cards with special features such as reward schemes, discounts on certain goods and services or rebate offers often have higher interest rates.

Balance Transfer Offers

You can get the full benefit of these offers by paying the transfer amount within the agreed upon period. If the entire amount is not paid before the end of the transfer period, the balance is often charged at the standard interest rate or the cash advance rate which can be much higher. Terms and conditions may be different for each balance transfer so make sure you understand what they are.

The Truth About Credit Card Limits

The use of credit cards is constantly increasing, but there are still many people who are against them and others who simply don't care about a credit card, but is it good to have a credit card? How convenient is it to go through life without one?

Due to the demand for credit cards in the world, the benefits they provide to people have increased. Many of these allow us to live more pleasurable experiences and save money, as well as being a safer method of payment than carrying cash.

Like any credit, cards have their advantages and disadvantages, and, to a great extent, their convenience depends on the particular needs and lifestyle of each person, so I will point out some of the main advantages and in the same way disadvantages you may have for the use of credit cards.

Advantages:

- You won't have huge amounts of cash in your wallet nor will you run the risk of losing your savings on that product you wanted to buy so much.

- You have a wide range of services that you can cover with the credit system. To make hotel reservations or rent a car is almost essential to have a credit card, as it acts as a guarantee.

- Immediate liquidity whenever you need it. If you use credit responsibly, a card guarantees that you will have money available when you need it.

- You have the possibility of extending credit cards to your relatives or associates for greater control of expenses.

- You can access the cash advance in times of hardship. Unfortunately, not all the loans on the market are so fast, sometimes you have to wait days for them to resolve, and in case of an emergency, that's not an option.

- Security against theft.

- Online purchases are instantly eligible.

The Internet has opened the doors to practically any type of commerce with just a few clicks. You can also pay for your services like water, electricity, telephone, internet by direct debit so that they are automatically charged to your card.

- Access large purchases on deferred payments without affecting your monthly expenses.

What happens when you suddenly need a new refrigerator or computer? There are thousands of low-cost used product options but what if you want a new one? If you don't have savings, you will probably have to use the credit offered by the store, that of small weekly payments that take years to pay off and with high-interest rates. If you have a credit card, you will probably find promotions of payments to months without interests so that you neither have to make a great disbursement that you did not have planned nor do you have to pay interests for your financing.

Disadvantages:

- You buy more on impulse. He's tempted to buy with the money that doesn't exist in his bank account.

- More interest is paid, depending on the number of installment to which a purchase is deferred.

- High-interest rates or many countries with no fixed term.

- Fees for handling plastic.

- If your credit history is impoverished due to delinquency, your quality of life will be affected by not being able to access future credit plans, which in turn impedes your goal of obtaining a mortgage, an auto loan, or even medical coverage.

Of course, all the above points will depend on the good use or misuse you give your credit card and of course, the simple fact of having a credit card implies that you must have a fixed monthly income or some income that serves as a support to have financial resources to cover the commitments made.

As you can see, a credit card has great benefits, whether you use it regularly for your everyday expenses or it's a backup in case of emergencies. It is also important to consider that if you are asked for credit history and you still don't have one, remember that the use of a credit card can help you build one.

Chapter 13. Personal or Business Credit Card?

A personal credit score will be between 300 and 850. A score in the high 700s will be an attractive customer for credit agencies. A high credit score can have many benefits. You can negotiate better deals, qualify for additional credit more easily, and be offered some of the best credit terms available. Business credit cards offer similar rewards to personal credit cards, but you will only get these if the business has a good credit score. Most of the rewards for business will be in the form of a cash back percentage on the purchases made with the business credit card. You are effectively saving money with every purchase. The business can often use the cash back to pay for reduced flight fares, which is highly beneficial if your employees need to travel for work.

Business credit card balances don't show on your personal credit unless you personally guarantee them or miss payments.

Therefore, any purchases made with a business credit card will not adversely affect your scores. Even if you max out your business credit card month after month, it will not hurt your personal credit score. Unfortunately, the balances you carry with your PERSONAL credit cards affects your scores more than almost anything else.

The Do's and Don'ts of Managing Your Credit

One of the most common things that I hear from people I meet and help is: Tell me what to do. That is actually a very powerful statement: "Tell me what to do." For one, it means that people have started to take the first steps towards improving not only their credit, but their lives as well. It also means that people trust me to help them.

DO: Always, always pay on time. Considering that your payment history is the biggest percentage when it comes to calculating your credit score, it is crucial that you make all payments punctually. If possible, make credit card payments before the reporting date.

DON'T: Be late or miss a payment; once again, payment history is one of the biggest components used when calculating your FICO Score. Making late payments can lead to serious consequences. You can be charged a late fee, your interest rates may rise, the late payment marking will be reflected on your credit report, and your credit score may sink.

DO: Watch your usage of available credit. Remember that utilization plays a big role in your credit scoring. If you have credit cards that are maxed out, your credit score will suffer.

DON'T: Max out any of your credit cards. If you have a few credit cards but one of them is your absolute favorite, try to spread out the usage. If one credit card is maxed out, don't be afraid to transfer balances so that you can meet the 30% mark. Also make sure that the credit card or cards with the higher limits get paid off first.

DO: Age your accounts. Simply, the older your accounts, the better. Recall that Length of History was a component of your credit scoring. Aging your accounts will help to improve your credit file and credit score.

DON'T: Close older accounts. I have seen many people make the mistake of closing older accounts because they do not use them anymore. It is far from a good idea to do this. Also try to avoid opening too many new accounts; this brings the age average down.

DO: Make sure to minimize new credit. You don't want to open up too many new accounts too fast. Doing so would affect the aging of your accounts as mentioned.

DON'T: Make too many inquiries. An inquiry is simply whenever you, or someone else, requests your credit file. There are two types of inquiries: a hard pull and a soft pull. A soft pull inquiry does not have the same potential for credit disaster as a hard pull possesses. A hard pull occurs when you request your credit file to apply for credit (credit cards, car, house etc.) A soft pull occurs when companies request your file in order to make you credit card offers and such.

DO: Mix up your accounts and add variety. If you were to submit a résumé to an employer, the more work experience and variety you presented, the more likely you are to be hired. By adding variety to your file, you are showing that you know how to manage your credit in more than one way.

The Secret to Success

The value of credit is highly underestimated and it is done so on purpose. If everyone knew the true value of credit and how to make it work for them, there would be an overflow of successful people and perhaps even more millionaires. The business of lending is one of the biggest industries on earth due to the trillions of dollars being exchanged at varying interest rates. The lower your credit score, the higher the interest rate; the higher the interest rates, the more you pay and the more they make. Saving 1% on an interest rate can be the difference in tens of thousands of dollars. It is clear to see that credit is important and valuable. But let's discuss how it can make you successful.

Making powerful investments in life, such as real estate or opening up a business can take tons of money and it can take more money than most people have available. This is where the value of credit comes in. With a good credit score, making investments without having the cash is extremely possible. When you build your credit file exactly the way it's supposed to be, it makes it so much easier for lenders to decide to loan you money no matter what type of purchase or investment you wish to make.

When it comes to opening a business, banks are willing to give small business startup loans to get a business off the ground, but it all depends on your credit score. They want someone who is guaranteed to repay the money, a Personal Guarantor. So no matter what you are doing: making a big purchase, starting up a new business, or being a real estate mogul, your credit will always be a major decision factor. This is the reason why credit is the secret to success and taking care of your credit can truly lead to the American Dream or at least financial stability. Many of the world's richest people were not born with money but made their fortune through knowledge and innovation.

Chapter 14. Keeping Your Score Healthy

Your credit report is a storyline of your credit life and it is used by potential lenders to determine whether they should provide credit to you. You should be very vigilant of your credit report and maintain it to ensure that a potential future lender will view your financial history favorably when it is time to lend you the credit you need.

Advantages of Having an Excellent FICO Credit Score

Periodic interest-free credit offers

Banks, like all other businesses, compete with each other for the same customers. To lure customers from their rivals, banks sometimes offer customers interest-free credit cards for a specified period. Look for such deals whenever you need to refinance your credit card debt.

Low-interest rate credit card offers

When you improve your credit score, lending institutions will be watching you. They know that with your improved credit score, their risk of doing business with you is lower. That is excellent news for them. They will, therefore, try to lure you into being their customer with low-interest credit cards.

Credit cards that offer you cash back

If you buy stuff worth a lot of money every month and you have a high/excellent FICO score, then lending institutions most likely already know about you. Their creative managers try to figure out ways to get some of that money into their cash registers. Cash back for your purchases is almost a sure way to snag you.

Credit Score Myths

Most people think certain things need to happen to have a great credit score. Most of these myths are wrong and affect their potential to have the highest score possible. Knowing what is true and what is a myth could save you years of mismanaged credit. Focus on reality and not on myths by going over some of the most common misconceptions shown below:

If you're 21 years of age or younger, you can't have a credit score above 700

Wrong. Your credit score is not age based and it does not take this criteria into account when calculating your score.

If I get married, my credit score will go down

Wrong, your credit score is independent to your spouse's score unless you have joint credit accounts in which case payment history and the amount of debt carried can affect you in a positive or negative manner. Your marital status is irrelevant.

If I pay off all my credit cards I will have an 800 credit score

Incorrect. Paying off your credit cards should increase your credit score but there are more factors to take into account when determining your credit score such as: length of credit history, credit mix, inquiries, debt capacity, etc.

If I check my credit online, it will go down

There are times when having your credit checked or when you check your credit that you're credit scores will not be affected. Normally, your credit score is affected when you apply for credit and your credit is pulled, not when you check your own credit.

If I lose my job, my score will go down

This is not correct. Your employment status is not linked to your credit and will not affect your credit score. If you are late on payments as a result of losing your job, this will result in a lower score. If you can keep making your payments on time your score will not go down.

If I make a million dollars a year, I will have a credit score above 750

No. Your credit scores are not affected by how much you make. Your salary can be $100 or $1,000,000, your score will not change. Managing your credit properly will affect your credit. Some people that are very wealthy can have low credit scores while someone who is getting paid minimum wage can have an over 800 credit score.

If I buy a house worth $700,000 and owe $600,000 my credit will be negatively affected because of the amount of debt I owe

This is not correct. Applying for a mortgage will lower your credit scores because they are being pulled to check your credit but the amount you owe is irrelevant. Your monthly payment can be $4,000 on your mortgage and your credit will not be affected. Once you start paying down your $600,000 loan, your credit will improve as a result of paying on time and lowering you debt. If you put 10% or 30% down payment on a house you buy, your credit will not be affected by this either since it is payment history based and will only be affected by your capacity to repay the loan.

If I move to another country my credit score will go down

It does not matter where you live, credit history and your credit score is based on your capacity to manage debt properly not on where you are. You can live in New York City, Miami, Seattle, Washington D.C., Los Angeles, Mexico, Germany, Australia, and your credit score will not be affected.

If I turn 80 years old I will no longer be able to improve my credit score

Wrong, age is not a factor when it comes to your credit and your credit score. If you live to be 120 years old, you can continue having great credit and a high credit score.

If I make a late payment on my credit card my score will drop to 300

Incorrect, assuming a score based on a late payment is not the way to assess your credit score as it can be slightly lower or it can drop much lower. There is no precise way to know exactly what your score will be.

If I apply for too many credit cards my score will go down

Correct. Credit inquiries lower your credit score by a small amount but when you continually apply for credit, your credit will be checked often and will result in a lower score.

Conclusion

Credit is significant for anybody's accounts. It gives an individual a history and reputation of their budgetary history. With credit, individuals can fund things for example, a house or a vehicle. At whatever point an individual has credit, it is significant that they use it shrewdly. A decent record as a consumer will empower them to get low financing costs on credits and get more cash. There are various things that individuals should remember when utilizing credit. They should do things, for example, take care of tabs on schedule, check their announcements, check their credit reports and furthermore maintain a strategic distance from the base installment propensity.

Dealing with your record is significant on the off chance that you need to ensure that you can acquire enough cash to purchase a house or a vehicle. It will likewise enable you to get the most minimal loan costs and set aside you cash thus. At whatever point you are hoping to deal with your credit, it will be imperative to ensure that you charge a sum that you can stand to pay back and take care of your tabs on schedule. This will enable you to build up and keep up a decent record of loan repayment and deal with your credit carefully.

www.ingramcontent.com/pod-product-compliance
Lightning Source LLC
Chambersburg PA
CBHW071419210526
45465CB00001B/462